INKLING

KIANA LIN

Inkling copyright ©2021 Kiana Lin.

All rights reserved. No part of this book may be used or reproduced in any manner whatsoever without the written permission of the author, save in the context of excerpts for reviews or education.

ISBN: 978-1-7363255-0-6

Written, edited, and produced by Kiana Lin

Cover design by Kiana Lin

www.creativeinklin.com

*To my family–those of blood and those who were found:
For always believing I was worth knowing,
and for challenging the times I've tried to keep others
from seeing deeper into my life.*

LISTEN

I am young but once.
I am not thoughtless, reckless.
I will not regret,
So I cannot leave this unsaid.

Time has me on a leash:
He leads me in circles,
Hoping I'll become dizzy,
Believing I am in charge.

What does it look like?
Feel like?
Why do you need me
To tell you about your world?
Are you so impressionable,
Swayed by my words?
If I told you it was the ocean–
The desert–
Would you see waves and sandy dunes,
Instead of the curl of the paper's edge?

Real innocence,
Shared laughter,
Happy dreams:
You speak of these things
As if they are gone,
Fled from your life and your thoughts,
Only to return
When memories are dredged ...
Are you so far gone
That you only sometimes
Recall the good of the past?
Have you none to expect,
To greet in the present?

Is this real to you
Or is it rehearsed, constant
Till you believe it?

You have so many words to say–
Wanting so desperately to be heard,
You drown yourself in nonsense.
Don't you realize the power in silence?
The eloquence of brevity?
The cosmos was sculpted–
Breathed into existence–
In mere sentences.

It's like giving up:
Betraying the magic,
That unassuming sparkle,
Which you once found
Glimmering
Deep within the mundane.

Regret–
Comprised of pride,
Drenched in control,
Stinking of fear...
Utterly lacking in
Self-awareness.

Thoughts become actions–
Follow through from the feelings–
So what is the point,
Really?

Life is for the longest haul,
Our futures must be built.
Yet a day full up of choices
Can lead to virtues spilt.

It's hardly named as rashness
When the actions that are made
Are daily picked and used again,
Despite the shining's fade.

And yet, even so, you know
There's something to be said
About the way we rush and run
To put each day to bed.

Our decisions do ever linger on,
Though night is close at hand.
The years are too unkind to those
Who'd make their lives as bland.

To live underwhelmed is truly that:
A reckless waste of time.
Why even now, my day's half spent,
In writing this worthless rhyme.

Who says our firsts are always
Lovely, lucky, light?
Can't we wallow in our darkness–
Lonely, lazy, listless . . .
Can't we be real?

We fill sinks with galaxies,
Send them swirling
Down the drain,
And in moments we dispose of it–
Our so-called magic.
All whilst ignoring
The ever fading beauty
That can be gained with a single step:
Out of doors and under the heavens,
Made especially for our wonder.
We trivialize and attempt to compress
What was created to be vast,
Limitless.
And we do the same to our stars.

Everything gone wrong,
Left to our own human devices,
The world what we make of it,
What we wish in our deepest–
Our darkest–
Moments of hubris.
And then we dare to ask
For the help we turned away.
We make demands and rail against
The One we scorned in the heights
Of our mortal delusions.

You imagine it
A thing of light and loveliness?
Can you picture
The distinctly crystalline sharpness,
Comprehend
The unfeeling, deadly wanting?
There is such terrible, horrific bitterness–
Joy
To be caught, grasped, strangled.
Perhaps
It is a cold, frightful sort of beauty,
If only you could stand to behold it,
Lingering
In the darkness.

Hypocrisy hides in humor,
Disguises barbed feelings
In clever wording and
Ringing tones of laughter.
But a closer look
Reveals the hurtful intent
That is fully rotten at the core.

Time,
Ever cruel,
Inconspicuous
In his passing, yet
Looming
At his reckoning.

Support is more than words.
The best of your intentions
Are not enough,
Never enough.
To save the day,
To endure the pain,
To come out ahead
And become whole–
Nothing less than action will suffice.
Sacrifice your all
On the altar of indifference,
Or step aside,
Watching from the sidelines
With your useless goodwill.

Clenched fist, an initial reaction,
Even so, a choice must be made:
Fingers curling, tighter still
Or, gently unfurling–
Salvation at hand.
Impossible
To let go,
Even
So.

Do not flood me
With your condolences.
Trash your *so sorry's*,
Hold your offers of help,
Wait with your sympathies,
Giving me time–
Let it hurt first.

For someone who sees the big picture,
You focus on the details, but
You still manage to miss out,
Ignoring the essence
Of a thing because
You want to see
Something that
Is not
There.
And so,
Subtlety
Isn't your strong suit.
You are blinded to
The root of the matter,
The why behind the reason.
Preferring your panorama,
Your lofty, lonely, birds-eye viewing.

Comforting words
For an uncomfortable time.
Where any progress is good progress,
Innovation, wonder, adventure–
They go to die,
Withering away under the shadow
Of imagined growth.
The rotting of roots:
When the nourishing water
Sits stagnant and kills the soul.

Forethought
Does not help,
Wisdom
Cannot negate the necessity,
And knowledge
Will not expose the emotions
When you are backed into the corner
And left
To decide in the final moments.

Heart pounding, rushing,
Thoughts clouding, claws emerging–
When all else fails, fight.

How disappointing
To care until brimming,
Overflowing,
Only to be met
With empty minds and dead eyes.
Incandescent,
Spoiling for war
Yet somehow losing:
An army of one against none.
There is no one awake enough
To know, to appear–
To realize they are the victors.

Oh, how exhausting...
Righting every wrong,
Fighting every battle,
Letting everything pierce
Your armor through.
All because you
Refuse to simply
Let it go.

There are only two options for you:
Move past it or get over it.
With both choices you must act,
Never settling or
Turning, going back.
To stay is to
Sink, to dwell
Will be
Death.

Malice or oblivion: Who knows?
Intention–the control thereof–
It separates mind and soul
Or binds them more closely.
Awareness, also,
The cutting edge
Upon which
Death, Life
Fall.

Frigid or scorching–
There's no half of heartlessness:
Only do or die.

Temerarious:
To wait, do nothing–stillness.
Pausing life is death.

You desire to be in control of
The here, the now, and the future.
You covet what you can't have,
Attempting to steal what
Was never meant for
Humans to own.
How could we
Even
Try?

We are afraid to endure,
Worrying about our futures,
Exhausting ourselves with waiting.
So much is lost to stretches of time,
That our most potent living
Is accomplished in little splices.

If bracing for a shout,
Can you even hear the whisper?
What is a nudge
When compared to a shove?
You search for fireworks,
Yet a candle is already at hand.
We are our own worst complications.
Inspiration is simplicity,
Waiting quietly to be noticed,
So ready to be useful,
If only we would look
Longer than a moment.

I can lead you
To stand in the light,
But all you will see
Is the darkness
If you refuse to simply
Open your eyes.

Has it passed you by?
Flown beyond the ear
And been lost,
Dying–
As all breath and sound
Must eventually do?
Or has it wormed its way inside,
Buried beneath the skin,
And lodged in heart and mind,
Eternal–
As words occasionally become?

Magic exists in the realm of wording.
Choose carefully
What spells you cast on others:
Known or unknown,
Phrases grow, fester, infect.
Speak life where you can,
Truth when you must,
And learn to hold death
Captive on your tongue,
Behind a white cage.

FEEL

Breathe, take it all in.
Is it better than before
You truly let go?

Life, experience,
In growing old we are forced
To know–be–too much.

I can't put my finger on it:
This slight inconvenience.
Nothing at all, but
A notion of imbalance,
The approaching doom.

What we want,
What we crave,
What we throw away
Without thought:
We beg for words–
We demand silence.

Loneliness
Is not a sudden feeling.
It is a hunter,
Stalking,
Creeping,
Enveloping.
It is a mist that surrounds us.
The silence that kills,
A beauty that blinds,
An enduring cold that drowns
Even the warmest sparks.

I don't know why,
Or how to make it right,
Or how to let this go.
I want it,
But at the same time,
I can't stand to be hurt any more.
So here I am,
Tethered so closely,
Refusing to strain my leash,
But aching to run.

Inner wilderness,
On the brink of tipping out.
A reaction, a non-reaction,
A breath and a hesitation.
Eternity
Suspended in a moment, a memory.
A choice and a fear,
A cry that cannot be retrieved.
The tidal wave
Caught and stilled by a thread.

My thoughts are better kept
Confined to pages,
Hand-written and then torn apart.
Scattered pieces of my being
Trapped in words.
My soul drained in swirls of ink.

Fantasy has its place, its right time,
But even a dream loses charm.
Eventually it fades,
The vision collapses,
And then you are left
To face demons.
Dose yourself–
Ready,
Real.

Procrastinating: As if there's time,
As if we are truly endless.
Wasting Time: Letting life pass,
Watching it slip away.
Regret: For the end,
Approaching still.
Death: It comes
For all.
Now.

Deeper than bone,
Thicker than blood.
Sunk within the soul,
Tangled inside the mind.
Little hints adding up
Behind eyelids squeezed tight,
Despite perfected misunderstanding.
I guessed.
I feared.
I felt.
I denied.

– I Knew.

I am being handed
Disappointment
After disappointment
After disappointment . . .
And yet,
I am not disappointed.
I have no time
To embrace a feeling
That is so
Useless,
Obvious,
Meaningless.
And yet, I am
Only human.

A thousand little cuts,
A million momentary thoughts.
Words like vampires descend–
Sucked dry of reason,
Empty and exhausted,
An endless assault.
The victim,
The perpetrator,
The judge and jury:
Only me.
Myself to blame,
To answer to.

Bad behavior is more than your self
Creeping out of your darkest depth,
The uglier parts displayed.
It is your shadow as
You cast your anger,
Your fear and hurt,
Looming there,
For all.
Seen.

For hope, stubbornness,
Pride that is our downfall, and–
Even still–our choice.

A choice–
Difficult when drenched in history,
Simple when a beginning.
A decision:
A continued legacy,
Or one last polite farewell.

Nothing more to give,
And yet all the more to lose
With just one word: Yes.

Individual:
When having the same idea
Means different paths.

Life happens slowly–
A moment here,
An hour there.
Still, somehow,
Before you've quite woken,
Sleep is already upon you.

Unremarkable days, we think,
Lost in oblivion.
Precious are those memories
In quiet moments of sadness.

So few options left,
No way out once it begins,
Just push ever on.

When does the pain end,
Does it become just too much–
Indiscernible?

Some days,
You won't want to talk about it at all,
Avoiding even the mention.
Other days,
It consumes you–
To the point that you
Have to let all the emotions out
And it's the only thing
You can think about.
Some days,
And someday's.

My mind overloading with memories,
Floating.
Missing you, my heart empties–
Sinking.

You–
Just out of sight.
My heart:
Gone from my chest.

Tears for you, only.
Love stays–slowly, slowly fades–
But hurt still remains.

Grief is like the ocean,
Swelling and dipping,
Twisting, receding soothingly,
Swirling round my ankles
Then cascading, overwhelming.
Leaving me bereft,
Tossing and sputtering,
As I finally emerge–
A sting in my eyes,
Heart pounding then freezing,
Limbs trembling,
Choking on halting breaths.
The taste of salt
Ever on my lips ...
And it begins again.

The ever present
Disconnect.
The fight to feel,
Removed.
Worthy of overcoming
Indifference.

Do you ever feel it?
Everything aches–
But not quite.
Exhaustion weighs heavy,
Yet restlessness prevails.
There is nothing here,
And still all you can do is remain.
Unsteady on your legs
While blood fizzes and bubbles,
Effervescent in your veins,
Static buzzing in your brain . . .
Perhaps if you move,
Think,
Or fall asleep quickly,
Something will shift inside,
Will quiet down.
If you stretch jelly limbs
Just far enough–
You can become strong,
Reach a place of peace,
Your body and mind
In sync once again.
For a time.
Do you ever feel it?

Perhaps I will, or
Perhaps, I can't ever be . . .
But for now I am

- Okay.

When you first began,
The choices you faced–endless.
Did you see it, whole?

LEARN

And so it comes
On the wind,
In the storm . . .
The welcome gloom–
The bringer of new life.

Choices, responses:
I am my own person.
Subconscious, purpose:
I will be my own reason.
Deliberate, accidental:
I can be a part.
Intonation, emotion:
I choose to love.
Connotation, logic:
I can be and I am

– The One That Breaks.

I am not and yet
I am, no?
I wait
And I have already begun.
I am in love
And I have hate.
Do your worst,
But be gentle with me.
I am, yes.

– Are You Ready?

Life requires context–
Without it,
We are devoid of grace.
And understanding is only found
Lingering in the background.

Loud and horrific curiosity,
Maybe sincere and quiet support,
Perhaps laughing dismissal,
Or a worshipful hunger:
How do you want the world
To approach the story of your life?

There is more,
We think.
We always think.

Can this be the end?
We wonder.
Always wonder.

We always expect.
We are always surprised,
Are always human.

How do you banish the darkness?
By allowing something to burn.
It's a short life,
But no less meaningful
For its brevity and beauty.

What gives us our purpose or our worth?
Is it the time spent on learning,
The distance travelled, even
A chance at fame, fortune?
Or is it perhaps
A connection,
A simple:
Hello
There!

A single question:
Will you risk mischief, ruin
For a glimpse of joy?

Even a tiny emotion
Speaks volumes.
What has sparked
Your cold heart?
What has struck
The hope of future flames?

There is more than now,
More than here, more than what was–
More choices to come.

Something shattered beyond repair
Can still cut–sharp and deep.
A change in purpose
Does not amount to uselessness.

Speak what must be applied–
And don't hold back.
But sprinkle it with understanding,
To ease the mouthful.

Tell me with your words
The things my actions can do
For reality.

Against all reason,
Becoming complicated is the easy path.
The difficult choice,
The backbreaking work:
To clear the way.
To simplify is the roughest route
At the fore,
Yet the least maintenance
In eventuality.
Peace is not inherent–
So what to do?
The only thing you can:

– Start Simply.

Wandering minds learn.
Worlds, cultures, hearts are found out,
Uncovered by thoughts.

Think between the lines.
What is heard, is understood,
　　Is something I feel.

Feelings,
A flood of words.
Emotions–
An ebb and flow.

It's on the wind's sigh,
A striped tail, a tiny croak:
Change is on its way.

Are you taking it in?
Are you appreciating this?
Each moment:
A singular, unrepeatable gift.

What is romance,
But the slight filtering of sunlight
Through the same leaves,
At the same time,
Every day?

– Repeatable

The breeze ruffling through the trees:
Do you hear it?
That burbling little laugh,
The crackling of embers,
A satisfying and breathy sigh,
The roaring of water beating the rocks:
Just now–
Right here–
Only for you.

Did you hear it?
Beating so quietly,
Thumping, pumping.

Can you feel it?
Firing down the pathways,
Sparking, igniting.

Will you miss it?
Uncurling like a cat,
Flying, expanding.

Are we not immortal?
Leaving behind a shell,
Unfurling, emerging.

There are moments
Where words fail,
Times when the only way to explain,
To express
The complete contentment within,
Is to loose the hum
That inhabits your chest.
The vibrations of which
Speak louder than any language
Could properly communicate.

Speak to me of abstract things:
The first inkling of love,
The last remnant of sleepy dreams,
The truth in the legend.

The dark brings magic.
What will you do with tonight,
Before daylight breaks?

Beat and breath, blood and tears, shine, shadow:
Words are thoughts set loose, wild, living.
Ink survives, conjures feelings,
Tongues slice through defenses,
Pages hold secrets.
We can be freed
By simple
Works of
Heart.

Wait right where you are, stand here, right now.
Take in this moment, be it good
Or your deepest, darkest time:
There is something to be
Gained, learned, and
Something worth your
Remembrance.
Even
Now.

You can stumble in pain,
Eyes clenched shut,
Praying against the fears you can't see,
The horrors you imagine.
Or you can walk in the wonder,
Feast your gaze upon the possibilities,
Accepting what lies before you–
The hopes you dream.

There is something beyond this,
The here and now
Hold me no longer:
For my spirit has searched ahead
To find my joy,
My happiness.
My hope is in the waiting,
The stillness.

A genesis
Is rarely laid bare,
Even to those
To whom those beginnings belong.
Discernment
Comes with the eleventh hour;
The journey always harried,
Yet the arrival
Is surreptitious in the end.

What you know is past;
What you see is what will be;
What you do is life.

A real hopefulness,
A tremulous thing, and still–
There is strength in it.

Joy is found
Skulking within change–
The struggle
That sweetens the wins.
Have you the will to search?

A quiet, warm glow,
A brilliant, knowing rightness–
Either way, equals.

It will always be,
It will never come to pass,
Hope always just is.

Each beat, drop of blood,
Moving for something, rushing–
Real, bright, ongoing.

My life is not mine,
Even the air is all You.
I'm on borrowed time.

You can do a thing
A thousand times,
But the magic of understanding
Is hidden–
In the least significant
Of the undertakings.
A random, unknowable
Moment.

The happy moments
Adding, building up to be
A filling, blessed life.

We measure with our
Eyes
The things that should be
Weighed
Only by our
Souls.

You don't remember it–
The memory
I took from your head
And placed within
My heart.

Words briefly whispered
Into sleepy ears, yet meant
To last a lifetime.

– Never Doubt that I Love You.

Of all the things you gave me,
This is the one that holds me, still–
Bringing your ghost to life,
Even if just for a moment.

True healing takes place
When the heart
No longer yearns for words
It could always beat without.

ABOUT THE AUTHOR

This is Kiana Lin's debut as an author, and she is–of course–still writing! To follow along on her journey and learn more, visit her website:

www.creativeinklin.com

Ever since she was a child, Kiana Lin has had a love of words. From her first made up phrase to fit her stubborn idea to learning to read out of a spiteful need for independence, she took in every bit of wordplay and storytelling craft that she could. Then, one summer, a creative writing assignment led to a late brainstorming session in her aunt's kitchen. That one night sparked the desire to create something she would enjoy reading for herself.

And then she never stopped.

www.ingramcontent.com/pod-product-compliance
Lightning Source LLC
Chambersburg PA
CBHW020911080526
44589CB00011B/538